The Hamps

Walmer RNLI lifeboat,

1975 – 1990

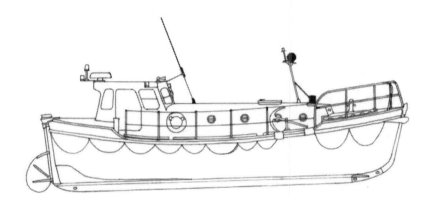

The story of her life

by Suzie Tubby

First Printing: 2014

ISBN 978-1-291-87100-5

Suzie Tubby
Langleigh Country House, Langleigh Road
Ilfracombe, Devon, UK EX34 8EA

Ordering Information:
Please contact Suzie Tubby Tel: 07961317088 or email info@lifeboattrips.co.uk

For the courageous, selfless men and women
of the Royal National Lifeboat Institution,
in the present, the past, and in the future.

To Idris

Thank you for sailing

with us !

Alec Rose in 1964

In 1973, Sir Alec Rose, famous for sailing single handed around the globe in his yacht *The Lively Lady*, began an appeal to raise funds for a new lifeboat, on behalf of the RNLI. The Portsmouth based greengrocer formed a committee and soon had not just the city of Portsmouth but schools and communities from around Hampshire involved in the fundraising.

A target was set of £50,000, with the cost of the boat being £95,000.

Sir Alec and his committee roused the people of Hampshire to support their cause, and within a few months of the appeal getting under way, over £30,000 (over £210,000 in today's money) had been raised.

It was reported in the Hampshire Telegraph on Thursday, September 26th, 1974, that a two day fete and lifeboat exhibition at H.M.S. Mercury, near East Meon, raised over £3,500, while in a separate report it was noted that a small infant school raised £12 with their fundraising efforts.

Whilst Rose and his committee were raising the funds for the new lifeboat, the boat itself was being built at William Osbourne's boatyard in Littlehampton, West Sussex. Osbourne, a car salesman turned boat builder, was instrumental in the design and building of the RNLI's first self – righting lifeboats, and over 100 lifeboats were built at his yard over the years, including the famous inshore lifeboat *Blue Peter 1*, funded with money raised by the popular children's television show.

Rother Class Lifeboats: The Mark II Oakley

The Rother class lifeboat, named for a tributary of the River Arun which runs through Littlehampton, came about in 1972, when the RNLI decided to redesign the Oakley class lifeboat. The 37' Oakley was a revolutionary design, using an ingenious water ballast transfer system for self – righting, designed by Richard Oakley, for whom the class was named. Twenty six of these lifeboats were built, with the majority being placed at stations where they were carriage launched and a few serving at stations with a slipway.

The Oakley class lifeboats had undergone several minor improvements to the original design over the years, all being incorporated into the newly built boats and many being retrofitted to older boats. The redesign in 1972 was with the dual objectives of providing enclosed accommodation for the crew and accommodating radar in the smallest of the RNLI's all-weather lifeboats.

There were many aspects of the new design that were similar to the Oakley, the hull shape was almost identical, despite being lengthened at the bow by six inches. The most obvious difference between the two boats was above the deck level, however, with the addition of the wheelhouse for the crew. This acted also as the entrance to the watertight cabin that housed both the engine room and the fore cabin, or survivors' cabin, which could also be accessed through a hatch in the roof.

The addition of this watertight superstructure served a second, more important purpose as well. Although the revolutionary water ballast system for self – righting had been successful in the Oakley design, it was abandoned in the design of the Rother in favour of a system whereby the watertight superstructure would be large enough to make the vessel incredibly unstable when capsized. The hollow roof of the wheelhouse would also aid with self – righting should the occasion arise, and in the hull, where there were water ballast tanks in the Oakley, there was now a double bottomed void. Should the hull be holed, this void would mean that the engine room would not be flooded.

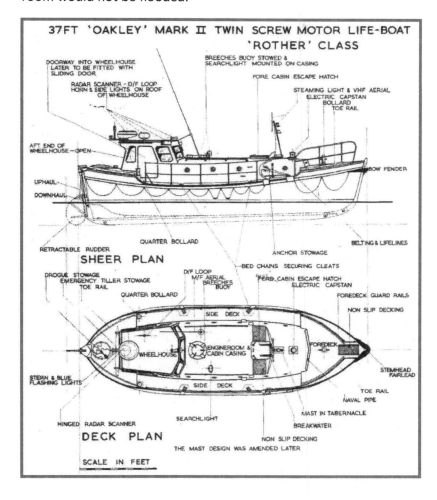

37FT 'OAKLEY' MARK II TWIN SCREW MOTOR LIFE-BOAT 'ROTHER' CLASS

SHEER PLAN

DECK PLAN

SCALE IN FEET

As these boats were to serve at locations with existing boathouses, they had to be built to fit the existing buildings, many of which had restricted headroom. Although the radar scanners, which would be fitted to the aft end of the wheelhouse roof, were the smallest available at the time, they still made the lifeboat too tall for many of the stations where they were due to be sent. This problem was solved by fitting the scanner onto a hinged bracket, which would swing down to stow the radar below the line of the roof.

The first Rother, *Osman Gabriel*, successfully completed self – righting trials on 9 September 1972. She was displayed at the Earl's Court Boat Show in January 1973 and entered service at Port Erin in July 1973. She was built at William Osbourne's yard in Littlehampton, the yard at which twelve of the fourteen Rother lifeboats, including *The Hampshire Rose*, were built.

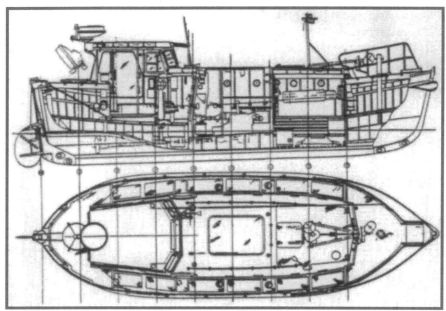

A cutaway drawing of the Rother class lifeboat

The Rother, which was a new design for lifeboats, was actually based on historically proven technology. In the 1800's, lifeboats were built with displacement hulls very similar to that of the new vessel. Although the lifeboats were not oar driven, as their nineteenth century counterparts had been, the twin engines that powered them were small 52 bhp affairs, capable of a top speed of only 8 knots. The Oakley lifeboats had been fitted with equally small engines, and the slow top speed of these vessels was no improvement on previous lifeboats.

When the 17 knot, 12 metre Mersey class was designed and developed in the mid-1980s, it became clear that the 37' Oakleys and Rothers would soon be replaced. In 1986, before even the prototype Mersey was completed, the RNLI made an announcement that gave an end date to the service life of these vessels. By 1993, every station that would operate an all-weather lifeboat would be served by one of the new fast lifeboats.

The result of meeting this target would mean that all the Oakleys and Rothers would be replaced or retired. In November 1993 the final Rother, *James Cable* of Aldeburgh, was replaced. The traditional double ended lifeboat design that had been used for over two centuries was finally retired, and a new, faster era of lifeboats had begun.

By September 1974, *The Hampshire Rose* was built, and ready to be launched from the boatyard at Littlehampton. Sir Alec, along with his wife, Lady Rose and members of the fundraising committee, were present for the launch. As detailed in newspaper articles at the time, Sir Alec presented a cheque for the first £10,000 installment to pay for the lifeboat at this ceremony.

Paying for the new 'Rose,' that's the people of Hants

Hampshire Rose by name, but this brand new self-righting lifeboat is destined for the straits of Dover, and was built in Sussex. The people of Hampshire, however, will be largely responsible for paying for the craft.

1974 is "The Year of the Lifeboat" marking the 150th anniversary of the foundation of the rescue service.

Hampshire organizers of the Royal National Lifeboat Institution launched an appeal fund that led up to the launching of the new lifeboat at Osborne's Yard, Rope Walk, Littlehampton on Monday last week.

The target was £50,000 — the cost of this self-righting Rother Class glass fibre boat.

Nationally the R.N.L.I. has set itself the target of replacing all lifeboats with self-righting models by 1980, which means buying 50 new boats at a total cost of £6m.

Sir Alec Rose, who is chairman of the Hampshire Rose appeal committee, was at Littlehampton for the launching to hand over the first £40,000 cheque to Major-General R. H. Farrant (Deputy Chairman of R.N.L.I. Management).

Latest news on the appeal fund is that £30,000 has already been found. East Hampshire Branch raised £1,000 through company and individual donations towards the cost of the twin 52 h.p. engines which will give the Hampshire rose an endurance of 180 miles at full speed of eight knots.

A two-day fete and lifeboat exhibition at H.M.S. Mercury, near East Meon, last week-end brought in more than £3,500.

Hampshire Rose will probably be stationed at Walmer near Deal where she will aid the work of saving lives around the treacherous Goodwin Sands.

Thanks to the R.N.L.I. 100,000 lives at sea have been saved in 150 years. Last year alone 1,002 people were rescued by the inshore boats and another 755 by the larger sea-going sort.

● In our picture Sir Alec and Lady Rose are offering the cheque for the initial £10,000 to Major-General Farrant flanked by two members of the Hampshire Rose Appeal committee Mr. Eric Pearman and Mr. Jack Chantler.

Article from the Hampshire Telegraph, Thursday 26th September 1974.

Sir Alec settles Hampshire Rose row

Sir Alec Rose made a peacemaking visit to Walmer, Kent, at the week-end to sort out the Hampshire Rose lifeboat name dispute. And he reports: "The crew say that they will be proud and happy to serve in a lifeboat called the Hampshire Rose."

Trouble started when the Mayor of Deal (Mr. Stuart Squares) told The News that some of his townsfolk were threatening to withdraw their lifelong support for the Royal National Lifeboat Institution.

They were annoyed because their new £65,000 lifeboat — for which Sir Alec is running the campaign to raise the money — was to be called Hampshire Rose.

Traditionally lifeboats stationed at Walmer — a suburb of Deal — have been called Charles Dibdin, after a founder secretary of the Institution.

Sir Alex, who had to visit Canterbury, to open a bazaar to raise money for the Hampshire Rose appeal, travelled on to Walmer to sort out the dispute.

DELIGHTED

"The coxswain told me that he is delighted with the Hampshire Rose," Sir Alec told The News, "He said that if there were any move to change the name from Hampshire Rose then there would be a mutiny among the crew.

"All of the crew agreed that they are absolutely delighted with the boat.

"I am so pleased that this has been sorted out. So many people in Hampshire have supported us generously — clubs, schools, and companies — that it is good to be able to tell them that their hard work and money has not been put in jeopardy.

"One or two people in the town may have objected to the name, but they were only a few. The lifeboat crew was as surprised and embarrassed by the objections as I was."

Following the launch at W.M. Osbourne, the lifeboat then underwent several months of trials. As one of the few beach launched Rother class lifeboats, *The Hampshire Rose* had required slight adaptations to her hull and superstructure to enable her to be launched safely and without damage being done. This meant that the sea trials she went through were not only focusing on her seaworthiness but also checking that the adaptations did not affect her performance to any measureable extent.

This was the first time that crew members from the Walmer station were able to come aboard their new boat, learning about the vessel and training in her operation. Crew members from other stations were also invited to visit during the trials, especially those who were due to have a Rother class at their lifeboat station.

On January 27th, 1975, *The Hampshire Rose* began her journey to Walmer from Littlehampton. Almost a week later, on February 1st, she arrived in Walmer, ready for the crew to really get to grips with the new boat and her technology before their current lifeboat, the *Charles Dibden (Civil Service No.32)* was taken off service. From February 3rd, 1975, *The Hampshire Rose* began her service life at Walmer Lifeboat Station, and along with her crew she made the waters of the Goodwin Sands a safer place for those who travelled upon them.

Lifeboat ceremony on June 1

On June 1st 1975, the official handing over ceremony took place at HMS Vernon, Portsmouth, which is now the site of Gunwharf Quays. The boat had already been in use at Walmer for some months, and several of the Lifeboat crew travelled with the vessel to Portsmouth for the occasion.

The ceremony was an unusual one, as it was neither a launching nor a naming ceremony, which were the traditional occasions that RNLI lifeboats were involved in. The launching had occurred in the previous September, and the official naming ceremony was due to take place in Walmer later in the summer.

The ceremony that took place on June 1st was planned specifically for *The Hampshire Rose*, to recognize Hampshire's interest in the lifeboat, as the area in which most of the money for the boat was raised. It was adapted from a naval ceremony, and following the blessing of the boat, Sir Alec Rose would officially hand the boat over to the crew of the Walmer station.

It happened that Her Majesty Queen Elizabeth the Queen Mother was returning from a trip to Guernsey, and was due to board a helicopter at HMS Vernon shortly before the 3.15pm ceremony. She agreed to delay her departure in order to meet Sir Alec and Lady Rose, members of the committee and their wives, and the meeting was planned for 2.45pm, with the ceremony to follow.

Her Majesty arrived on the Royal Barge, and, stepping ashore, stumbled a little, dropping her handbag into the water between the yacht and the pontoon. Lieutenant Hugh Slade, the Royal Barge

Officer, was more than ready to save the day. Ignoring the danger that he might become caught between the barge, rolling in the swell, and the pontoon he had laid down upon, he leant right over into the water and fished out Her Majesty's handbag.

He was said to have looked slightly embarrassed as Her Majesty thanked him, and her lady in waiting emptied the sea water out of the bag, before he returned to his station and Her Majesty went on to meet the reception party, then boarding her helicopter for her onward journey.

Lieutenant Hugh Slade can be seen prone on the pontoon as he fishes out Her Majesty's handbag.

The Queen Mother meets Sir Alec and Lady Rose (right) on her short visit to H.M.S. Vernon, Portsmouth.

Following the departure of Her Majesty and her entourage, the handing over ceremony was ready to begin.

Free tickets had been available to supporters for some weeks prior to the day itself, resulting in a crowd of around 500 people watching the event. The fundraising committee and their families were present, as were civic heads from Portsmouth, Havant, Gosport and Fareham and several naval dignitaries from H.M.S. Vernon.

A maroon exploded high above the crowd to signal both the launch of the proceedings and the end of over two years of campaigning, effort and generosity by the people of Hampshire. Almost £70,000 had been raised under the leadership of Sir Alec Rose, a figure far exceeding the initial £50,000 target and being more than anyone could have hoped for.

Speaking at the ceremony, the joy Sir Alec felt was clear to everyone present.

"This is a splendid occasion, and I am tremendously thrilled and proud to see her in the basin looking so smart and trim," he said. "I know the crew are thrilled with the boat. They have taken her to sea in a variety of weathers, and she handles beautifully."

Sir Alec made a point of thanking Hampshire's schoolchildren for their part in the fundraising. He explained that although the £50,000 target seemed like a lot of money when the appeal began, it had been exceeded by £18,000, and that the majority had been raised in small amounts by individuals and clubs, but particularly schools. He was quoted as telling the crowd that; "We are deeply grateful."

Following his speech, Sir Alec was praised by the Earl of Malmsbury, Lord Lieutenant of Hampshire, for his "splendid leadership" as Chairman of the Appeal Committee, before he officially handed over *The Hampshire Rose* and the cheque for the funds to Vice-Admiral Sir Peter Compston, Chairman of the RNLI Fundraising Committee. Sir Peter then presented Sir Alec with an inscription on vellum recording his election as an honorary Life Governor of the RNLI. Mr. E. Pearman, Vice-Chairman of the Appeal Committee; Mr. J. Chantler, Secretary; and Dr. P. Cameron, Treasurer; Sir Peter presented statuettes of lifeboatmen in thanks for their work.

Sir Peter ended his presentation by addressing the crowd, telling them that it was through the hard work and dedication of volunteers such as those involved with *The Hampshire Rose* appeal that the RNLI was able to maintain its lifeboat fleet at a cost of £5 million a year. He thanked the people of Hampshire for their generosity, which would enable the Institution to maintain a voluntary service "so respected by the people of this country and so greatly admired by our friends in Europe."

To end the ceremony, the Provost of Portsmouth; the Very Reverend Michael Nott; led the crowd in Drake's Prayer, and then performed the Final Blessing of the lifeboat.

O Lord God, when thou givest to Thy servants to endeavour any great matter, grant us also to know that it is not the beginning, but the continuing of the same unto the end, until it be thoroughly finished, which yieldeth the true glory; through His for the finishing of Thy work laid down His life, our Redeemer, Jesus Christ.

Drake's Prayer

Once the events of the day were over, *The Hampshire Rose* was ready to return home to Walmer. Prior to the handing over ceremony, she had been at Denton Ship repairers, Otterham Quay for some cosmetic work, and then travelled to Portsmouth for the ceremony itself.

The crew that travelled on passage with her then took the opportunity to do some sea trials and crew training, meaning that following the June 1st ceremony they finally arrived back at Walmer on June 26th.

For the vessel *Shamrock*, this was excellent timing on the part of the crew. She got in to trouble and was saved, along with her two crew and their dog, on June 29th. This was the first of the services performed by *The Hampshire Rose* during her fifteen years at Walmer.

The naming and dedication ceremony for *The Hampshire Rose*, held at Walmer Lifeboat Station on September 6th, 1975, was an exciting event for the town. The lifeboat had been in service at the station for seven months at that time, and had been launched on service three times, saving three souls.

The ceremony itself was a traditional one, led by the Bishop of Southampton, The Right Reverend John Kingsmill, who was assisted by the Vicar of Walmer, the Reverend Peter Hammond, M.A. It began at 3pm with the National Anthem, after which the Patron of the Goodwin Sands and Downs Branch, General Sir Norman Tailyour K.C.B., D.S.O. welcomed the guests, including Sir Alec and Lady Rose, along with members of *The Hampshire Rose* Fundraising Committee, and opened the proceedings.

Photograph showing The Hampshire Rose prior to the start of the naming ceremony.
Photo donated by Mr. P. O'Sullivan.

Mr. Michael Pennell, Eastern District Inspector of Lifeboats, followed the welcome from General Tailyour by describing the lifeboat for the congregation. Lady Norton, M.B.E., a member of the Committee of Management of the RNLI, then delivered the lifeboat to the care of the Walmer Branch for use on the Walmer Lifeboat Station. The lifeboat was accepted by Mr. Norman Cavell, Honorary Secretary of the Goodwin Sands and Downs Branch, on behalf of the Branch and Walmer Lifeboat Station.

SERVICE OF DEDICATION

Minister :   Let us pray
All :   Our Father which art in Heaven . . .
Minister :   Let us give thanks :

For the work of the Royal National Life-boat Institution; For the countless men and women who, down the years, have made this work possible; For the work of past boats and crews; For the work of our present crew; For the work of those who help ashore.

Let us pray for the Walmer Life-boatmen.

O LORD JESUS CHRIST, who on the Sea of Galilee did'st still the storm and bring Thy disciples safely to the land. Prosper, we pray thee, the skill and courage of our Life-boat crews in facing fog, storm and every peril of the deep. Preserve them both in body and soul, in all times of danger be their defence and bring them to the haven where they would be, through Jesus Christ our Lord.   *Amen.*

Extract from the order of service for the naming ceremony at Walmer Lifeboat Station on 6th September 1975.

Following this official delivery to the Lifeboat Station by the Institution, the Service of Dedication took place, beginning with the Lord's Prayer, and continuing with thanks and prayers for the work and people of the RNLI and Walmer Lifeboat Station.

The Junior Band of the Royal Marines, under the direction of W.O. (Bandmaster) J.L. Gould, L.R.A.M., provided the accompaniment as the choir and congregation then sang the hymn 'Eternal Father, strong to save'. The lesson, St. Matthew, Chapter 8, verses 23 – 27 was read, and next came a hymn, 'The waters from the shore display' written specially for the occasion by Reverend Hammond.

The Dedication of *The Hampshire Rose* Lifeboat was performed, and the final hymn, 'Amazing Grace' sung, before the Blessing.

The moment then came that the crowds had all been waiting for. Fanfares were played by The Herald Trumpeters of the Depot Royal Marines, under the direction of the Corps Bugle Major, W.O.2 J. Satchwell, and Lady Rose officially named the new Walmer Lifeboat as 'The Hampshire Rose'.

HYMN :   "The waters from the shore display"   *(Tune: Abridge)*.

The waters from the shore display
High waves and angry seas;
The ships within the harbour stay
And wait the wind to ease.

But some still move upon the sea
And find it running high;
They look for shelter but they see
No anchorage nearby.

Then is the danger and the shock
Hull hits and scrapes the sands,
Then firmly settles in a lock
Not made by human hands.

No movement now; and yet the waves
Still move, and strike and smash
Upon the ship, which now behaves
As men beneath the lash.

Now is the crisis, now despair;
The men look through the rain
To see if any help is there
To bring them home again.

And there's a boat; and now its light
Appears and disappears;
Hope rises at this welcome sight
And quietens unsaid fears.

Lord God, save those who travel through
High waves and angry seas.
Give strength to those who make the crew
To rescue such as these.

*(Verses specially written by
Reverend P. Hammond, M.A.,
Vicar of Walmer)*.

DEDICATION OF THE LIFE - BOAT

To the honour and glory of Almighty God and for the noble purpose of rescuing those in peril on the sea, we dedicate this Life-boat, in the Name of the Father and of the Son and of the Holy Ghost.   *Amen.*

The hymn written by Reverend P. Hammond, M.A., Vicar of Walmer, and the Dedication of the Lifeboat.

She was launched down the baulks on the beach into the sea, amid music and cheers, and made her way towards the Ramsgate and Boulogne lifeboats, which had made the journey to Walmer to salute the new vessel. A circular course was taken, and soon she had returned to the beach to be winched back up onto her turntable.

The following five photographs were kindly given to us by Mr. P. O'Sullivan, of Ramsgate, Kent, who was present at the naming ceremony on Saturday, September 6th, 1975.

The Herald Trumpeters of the Depot Royal Marines at the naming ceremony

Mr. O'Sullivan recalls:

'For September, it was an unusually warm day, and the Royal Marine Depot Bandsman on the right of [the photo] had to stand down and be revived with water shortly after I took the photo, much to the amusement of his colleagues and the withering look of the Corps Bugle Major! At least the RNLI crew were sympathetic!'

And she's off! The Hampshire Rose makes her way down the baulks into the sea, much to the delight of the waiting crowds

Returning to the beach for recovery, with the shore crew standing ready.

The Hampshire Rose had an active service life at Walmer RNLI lifeboat station, carrying her crew to many a rescue and safely home again. She was one of only a few lifeboats to be beach launched, with chains holding her fast to her turntable until the moment of launching, when she went sliding down into the sea over oiled wooden baulks, also known as 'skids'.

The Hampshire Rose poised and ready for launching on her cradle at Walmer Beach

The process for launching the lifeboat was, in theory, a simple one.

The lifeboat crew, along with shore crew and everyone in town who wanted to come along and watch, would be alerted to the imminent launch by the sound of the maroons firing. Crew would drop whatever it was they were doing at the time and rush to the lifeboat station, where they would get briefed and kitted up, before climbing the ladder to board *The Hampshire Rose*.

The chains would be released, and she would begin the slide towards the sea. Even at high tide, there was still quite a distance of beach for the lifeboat to travel before hitting the water.

The wooden baulks, oiled regularly and looked after well, meant that the lifeboat could slide over the shingle relatively smoothly. It was still not the easiest ride, however, and at one time, a crew member was heard to remark that it was like sliding a sled over a series of molehills.

(left) The Hampshire Rose as she left her turntable heading down towards the wooden baulks towards the sea.

The crew members to the left of the picture (right) needed to move quickly to avoid the fast moving vessel – she weighed in at over 13 tons!

(left) The soft shingle that makes up Walmer beach meant that the baulks were essential for the lifeboat to slide into the water. Without them, it would come to a complete standstill. On this occasion a couple of the baulks had moved out of place, but the momentum of the lifeboat was enough to get her far enough along to slide over the rest into the water. No doubt the running crewmen in the previous picture were attempting to put the baulks back in the right place before launch – and were just a little slower than they hoped to be.

Photos by Basil Kidd

However uncomfortable the launch, the crew of *The Hampshire Rose* always did their duty, giving aid to vessels in distress and saving lives on the treacherous Goodwin Sands.

Being so close to the shipping lanes of the Straits of Dover, it is unsurprising that many of the vessels that the lifeboat went to the aid of were commercial vessels. However, many pleasure craft also found themselves caught out by the tide and by the shifting sands, and it was a relief to all to know that the Walmer lifeboat was nearby.

Training exercises were regularly carried out by the crew of *The Hampshire Rose*, and due to their location and the wide range of vessels that they might have to deal with, whenever the chance came to train with other craft they took it.

The Hampshire Rose (left) during a training exercise with the Dover lifeboat, the Thames class 'Rotary Service' and a cross-channel hovercraft. Photo from RNLI Archives

*The Hampshire Rose during a training exercise with an
RAF Search and Rescue Wessex Helicopter.*

*The helicopter crew man and the 'casualty' are being winched from the deck
of the lifeboat to the helicopter as if in a real emergency.*

Photo by Basil Kidd

Preparing to return to the beach for recovery. A fantastic aerial shot of the lifeboat as she powers through the waves.

Members of Walmer's shore crew recovering the lifeboat.

Photos by Basil Kidd

Photo showing recovery of the Hampshire Rose on Walmer beach.
The shore crew are being given a helping hand by many willing members of the public

Recovery of the lifeboat was, as it is with most current all-weather lifeboats, a far more labour intensive process than the launch.

Once the boat had launched from the turntable, it was manually turned 180 degrees and locked back into place, to be ready for the vessel's return. The position of the baulks would be checked, and any that had shifted out of place moved back.

When the lifeboat returned to the beach, she would be winched up the baulks by an electronic winch on the turntable. The shore crew would be required to attach the winch wire to the bow of the lifeboat. Once she was finally settled on the turntable, the work continued. The chains that held her in place at the bow would be attached, before the turntable was once again turned by 180 degrees, ensuring that when next the lifeboat needed to be launched, she would be facing bow to the sea in readiness. The stern chain, fixed into the ground some feet behind the boat, was attached, and *The Hampshire Rose* was then secure. Crew members would clean her down and refuel her, making her ready for action once again.

(above) Members of the Walmer volunteer lifeboat crew who served aboard the Hampshire Rose, photo c.1980

(below) Members of the Walmer lifeboat shore crew. The three ladies in the picture began their time at Walmer lifeboat doing their Duke of Edinburgh award, and later joined up as shore crew. Both photos by Basil Kidd

Lifeboat's record

SINCE The Hampshire Rose went on service at Walmer Lifeboat Station two years ago, her crews have saved 43 people and one dog during 29 launches. They have also saved and towed to safety a variety of craft of an estimated value between £75,000 and £80,000.

This weekend a dozen members of the Hampshire Rose Appeal Committee and their yachtsman president, Sir Alec Rose, visit Walmer to mark the second anniversary of the naming ceremony of The Hampshire Rose in September, 1975.

In this Silver Jubilee Year The Goodwin Sands and Downs Lifeboat Station also celebrates the 25th birthday of the formation here of its Ladies' Lifeboat Guild in 1952, which has since raised about £27,000 towards the upkeep of the Walmer Lifeboat Station.

On Saturday evening, the Station Branch Patron, Gen.

Sir Norman Tailyour, supported by many local Lifeboat enthusiasts, holds an anniversary reception in Deal Castle to mark these two local birthdays.

Among those attending will be the chairman of the District Council (Cllr. George Aslett), the chairman of Kent County Council (Cllr. Alistair Lawton), the Town Mayor and Mayoress of Deal (Cllr. and Mrs. Alec Greenway-Stanley), the Town Mayor and Mayoress of Ramsgate and a number of Foundation and early Guild Committee members.

September 8th, 1977

A small selection of articles about the life saving activities of The Hampshire Rose during her time as Walmer RNLI lifeboat. These articles are all from the East Kent Mercury, the local newspaper covering the Walmer area.

Walmer Lifeboat saves 4 from yacht

WALMER Lifeboat towed a Dutch yacht—twice its tonnage—to safety on Tuesday. The 44ft steel-built Hendrick Jan had broken down and was drifting helplessly along the outer edge of the Goodwin Sands in heavy weather, with four people on board.

Cox'n Bruce Brown had to take The Hampshire Rose across the Sands well to the south because of low water, and Cyril Williams was put aboard the yacht.

A small coaster had gone to the yacht's assistance and put a line aboard to hold her clear of the sands. The yacht was towed into Dover Harbour.

MINUTES

Afterwards Bruce Brown and Cyril Williams told the "East Kent Mercury:" "The master of the coaster said the yacht would have struck the Goodwins within minutes of her May-Day call. Her engine had failed and his anchor would not hold in the running sea.

"He was getting nearer and nearer to the breaking surf over the Sands."

When the lifeboat went alongside to take over the tow, she was rolling badly and the rail stanchions were damaged.

The Dutch yacht had two men and two women on board and had sailed from Dunkirk that day.

June 7th, 1979

Lifeboat launched in a gale

In a southerly gale and rough seas the Walmer Lifeboat The Hampshire Rose, was launched on Wednesday afternoon last in answer to red flares just visible in rain squalls about three-quarters of a mile off the pierhead.

With Second Coxswain Cyril Williams in command, the lifeboat was quickly away and was alongside the casualty in 11 minutes. She was the local motorboat Sea Hooker, with a crew of three on board out net fishing, who had broken down with a fouled propellor.

She was quickly taken under tow for her beach plot near the Timeball Tower.

Because of the sea conditions along the beach, a number of the lifeboat's shore helpers, at Second Coxswain Williams' request, went to Deal to aid in the beaching of the casualty.

They then returned to Walmer for their usual job in the beaching and recovery of the lifeboat which was afloat for 50 minutes.

December 24th, 1980

Lifeboats saved 18

EIGHTEEN lives were saved by both the inshore and offshore lifeboats at Walmer in the year ending November, 1981.

The Hampshire Rose was called out 21 times, during the year, while the inshore lifeboat answered 11 calls between April and September, 1981.

Mr Norman Cavell, secretary of the RNLI Goodwin Sands and Downs branch, told members at the annual meeting in Deal Town Hall on Saturday, that a total of 2,210 people had been rescued by the branch since its inception in 1856.

The inshore lifeboat had rescued 167 people since it was introduced in 1964.

Mr Cavell said that more than 1,000 people were rescued by lifeboats round the British coastline in 1981. He also added that the cost of running the RNLI in 1982 was estimated at £16 million.

The treasurer, Mr John Hopper, said financially the branch was in a healthy position, with a balance of almost £9,000. The Ladies Lifeboat Guild raised £4,000, while donations totalled £2,779.

It was reported that the RNLI management committee had decided to introduce a 20-year service badge for lifeboat crew members and shore helpers.

The award would be a lapel badge, with recipients' surnames and initials inscribed on the back. One person who already qualified for the award was Walmer's head launcher, Mr Leslie Coe.

Mr Cavell said that the public response to the Penlee disaster fund had been considerable.

The Ladies Lifeboat Guild raised a large sum of money while the Walmer crew and shore helpers collected £100 before Christmas. One crew member collected more than £100 in a day, the Sandown Castle Hotel raised £145, while the Town Mayor's disaster fund totalled almost £250.

At the meeting, branch chairman Mr Jack Lewis was presented with a management committee silver badge, by the president, Sir Alec Rose, in recognition of his services to the RNLI. Mr Lewis also received an MBE in the New Year Honours list to mark his services to the National Coal Board.

Highlight of the year for the Goodwin Sands and Downs branch was the visit to the station in October by the Archbishop of Canterbury, Dr Robert Runcie.

Mr Lewis has been re-elected branch chairman and Mr Peter Broady, vice-chairman.

30

During *The Hampshire Rose*'s years of service, the Walmer RNLI volunteer crew also performed actions that were considered worthy of special merit by the RNLI.

In 1977, Coxswain Bruce Brown was awarded a Bronze Medal by the Institution for rescuing the four crew from the sinking cabin cruiser *Shark*, along with the Second Coxswain, who had become trapped in the cabin of the vessel.

THE LIFEBOAT

Cox'n Bruce Brown, depicted on the sign for public house 'The Lifeboat' on The Strand, Walmer. The pub had been renamed in 1976 to honour the local lifeboatmen.

Previously named the 'True Briton', it had been used by generations of Walmer's lifeboatmen, and it is said that survivors were often taken into the bar to be given dry clothes and refreshment.

In 1991, this new sign replaced the original 1976 sign, which had shown Harry Brown, former Walmer coxswain (and Bruce's uncle) on one side, and The Hampshire Rose on the other. The reverse of Bruce's sign has the (then) new inshore Atlantic 21, which replaced the Hampshire Rose at Walmer in 1990.

Cox'n Brown was also awarded a framed Letter of Thanks, along with Second Coxswain / Assistant Mechanic Cyril Williams, in 1978, for refloating the vessel *Elmela* off the Goodwin Sands. The rescue had taken place on December 10th of the previous year, in total darkness, force six to seven winds and heavy rain.

The lifeboat was launched in response to reports of ship's lights in the vicinity of the East Goodwin buoy, shortly before 11 pm. There were waves breaking over the boat, forcing the crew to reduce speed and making navigation and handling very difficult. The radar had developed a fault and so was unusable, meaning that every bit of the knowledge and skill of the crew was necessary to navigate the treacherous Goodwin Sands.

Arriving at the casualty vessel, *Elmela*, a Greek cargo ship, the lifeboat found her anchored on the Sands, with a heavy list to starboard and a crew of twenty five on board. Skillfully taking *The Hampshire Rose* alongside the stricken vessel despite the extreme condition of the sea, Coxswain Bruce Brown was able to get Second Coxswain Williams aboard.

The master of the *Elmela* declined offers to order tugs or to evacuate the crew, and so the lifeboat stood by as the tide ebbed.

At 4.59 am, Ramsgate's Waveney lifeboat, *Ralph and Joy Swann*, arrived to assist *The Hampshire Rose*, and after the two Coxswains agreed that *Elmela* was firmly settled until the next rising tide, the Walmer lifeboat left to return to her station, leaving Second Coxswain Williams aboard the casualty vessel.

Ralph and Joy Swann, Ramsgate's Waveney class all-weather lifeboat

Arriving at the beach at Walmer at about 7.15 am, there was to be no rest for the crew. The lifeboat was recovered, then refueled and re-launched at 8.45 am. With the wind and sea conditions having become slightly more moderate, and the winter sun having risen, the journey back to the scene was far easier, and by the time *Elmela* began to move with the rising tide at 9.15 am, *The Hampshire Rose* had rejoined the Ramsgate lifeboat.

The two lifeboat crews worked together to run a line from the ship's bow to the *Ralph and joy Swann*, and the casualty was pulled clear of the shoal area upon which she had become stranded.

Escorted by the Ramsgate lifeboat, she then made for Margate Roads.

By 10 am, Second Coxswain Williams had been taken aboard *The Hampshire Rose* again, and by midday she had returned to station to be recovered, refueled and made ready for service once more.

Framed letters of thanks, signed by Major-General Ralph Farrant, Chairman of the Institution, were sent to Coxswain Brown and Second Coxswain Williams for this service. The Ramsgate crew were similarly honoured, with letters signed by the RNLI Director, Captain Nigel Dixon being sent to Second Coxswain / Assistant Mechanic Derek Pegden and crew member Anthony Read of the *Ralph and Joy Swann*.

The Hampshire Rose and her crew welcomed dignitaries during her time in service. This visit of the Archbishop of Canterbury, Dr. Robert Runcie, was detailed in magazine 'The Lifeboat' in the winter edition 1981 / 82

He was taken out for a trip aboard The Hampshire Rose, and this picture by Basil Kidd shows Bruce Brown, volunteer Coxswain, introducing Dr. Runcie to members of the crew: left – right: Head Launcher Les Coe, crew members Denis Brophy and Paul Johnson

His Royal Highness, Prince Edward, Duke of Kent aboard the Hampshire Rose during a visit to Walmer lifeboat station.

HRH The Duke of Kent has been President of the RNLI since 1969.

Photo by Basil Kidd

The 1986 announcement by the RNLI that all its all-weather lifeboats would, by 1993, be the new fast boats, meant that the days of *The Hampshire Rose* were numbered. The decision whether Walmer would receive one of the new all-weather boats to replace their well-loved Rother would be down to the Coastal Review board, who assess the needs and capabilities of each RNLI lifeboat station every five years.

Lifeboat to be replaced

THE days of the Hampshire Rose seem numbered.

The famous Walmer lifeboat is in for a refit.

but with the RNLI committed to providing updated craft to all its stations by 1993, its future must now be in doubt.

What will replace the 14-year-old lifeboat is also in the balance.

The Wrother Class, to which the Hampshire Rose belongs, is no

longer on the building programme. The alternatives are a large long range inflatable with an all-weather capability, and the smaller inshore variety.

During the last year the Hampshire Rose has had only three call-outs, while the inshore inflatable has been been called out 12 times.

Said Terry Crowther, secretary of the Walmer Lifeboat: "The Coastal Review Committee has been here and its replacement was discussed.

"Ideally we would like a fast carriage boat which is the only replacement that can be operated off the beach. We feel a good case can be made for it.

"But we accept it is up to the RNLI. We are part of a national lifeboat service. We are not running our own little empire here.

"There is no infighting. We understand exactly what the situation is, and we will operate whatever we get as enthusiastically as we do now."

Whichever way the decision goes the RNLI has stated that Walmer will remain an all year round lifeboat station.

Is it the end of the line for the Hampshire Rose?

An article from the East Kent Mercury, October 19th, 1989

35

The RNLI's decision was that Walmer lifeboat station would no longer operate an all-weather lifeboat. Instead, the current D-class inshore lifeboat would be joined by the B-class Atlantic 21 *U.S. Navy League*. Since its arrival in 1964, the inshore lifeboat had only been on service during the summer months, but now both the Atlantic 21 and the D-class would be operational all year round.

As Walmer lifeboat, *The Hampshire Rose* had been launched on service 132 times, saving 57 lives and aiding many more.

The ceremony to send her off, on May 6th, 1990, was even more popular than the naming ceremony had been fifteen years previously. The lifeboat had more than proved herself to the people of Walmer and Deal, and it was an emotional time for many as they said goodbye, not only to the boat herself but also to the classification as an all-weather station.

Dressed for the occasion, The Hampshire Rose sits upon her cradle at the top of the beach for her last few hours at Walmer lifeboat station, ready for the ceremony that would precede her final launch.

top (left to right):

(top left): Walmer's new inshore lifeboat, the B-class Atlantic 21, James Burgess, waited in the water to pay her respects. Dover's Thames class lifeboat, Rotary Service, was present, also dressed overall for the occasion, as part of a fleet of boats that were gathered to escort The Hampshire Rose on the first part of her journey.
(top right): During the service.
(right): The Hampshire Rose waits on her turntable to be launched down the beach for the final time.

These pictures (and on previous page) used with the kind permission of Mr. B. Beer.

bottom (left to right):

(left): The lifeboat splashes down into the water.
(right): The crew wave to the thousands of onlookers as The Hampshire Rose leaves Walmer for the last time as an RNLI lifeboat.
These photos kindly donated by Mr. C. Varrall.

May 6th 1990, the day of the sending off ceremony, arrived with bright sunshine over Walmer. Thousands of people headed for Walmer beach, surrounding the lifeboat and wedging themselves onto every inch of the sand. Joining the locals were officials from RNLI headquarters at Poole, branch members from all over Kent and representatives from the coastguard service. Margate, Ramsgate and Dover RNLI lifeboat services sent representatives to the event, and most of the people involved at Walmer lifeboat were present to see their all-weather lifeboat off.

As cameramen perched on all available spaces ready to the capture the Hampshire Rose final launch, crowds mass onto the beach to give the craft a royal send-off.

Photographs (this and next page) by Basil Kidd for the East Kent Mercury, Monday 10th May 1990

Guests of honour included Sir Alec and Lady Rose, Lieutenant-Colonel Richard Dixon, Commandant of the Royal Marines in Deal and Mrs. Tricia Dixon, and Councillor Mrs. Marianne McNicholas, Mayor of Deal.

Reflecting the naming ceremony in 1975, the Junior Band of Royal Marines entertained the huge crowd with appropriately sea related tunes. Then the Vicar of Walmer, the Rev. Bruce Hawkins – also the Lifeboat Chaplain – conducted a short service, in which he gave thanks for the service that *The Hampshire Rose* had provided during her fifteen years at Walmer.

Vicar of Walmer, the Rev Bruce Hawkins, lifeboat chaplain, who conducted a short service before the Hampshire Rose was finally launched from the beach.

The ceremony included two important presentations by Sir Alec Rose. Volunteer Head Launcher Les Coe, who had served Walmer lifeboat for 22 years, was presented with a Royal Doulton statuette of a lifeboatman, on behalf of the crew and shore helpers, for his efforts as Head Launcher. Sir Alec also presented *The Hampshire Rose* book of donors to Mike Pennell, staff officer of the RNLI operations team. This book, with details of all those involved in the appeal masterminded by Sir Alec, was to go on display at RNLI headquarters in Poole.

Sir Alec Rose, on the left, presents the Hampshire Rose book of donors to Mike Pennell, RNLI staff officer, operations. The book will be on permanent display at the RNLI headquarters at Poole, Dorset.

To close the service, the thousands of people present joined in the singing of *For Those in Peril on the Sea*, and then it was time to launch the lifeboat. Head launcher Les Coe and chief Mechanic Bruce Brown had the honour of firing the final two maroons from the shore, and then *The Hampshire Rose* was off. With everyone present cheering and waving, the chains were released one last time, and the lifeboat slid over her baulks into the sea.

The Dover and Ramsgate lifeboats waited, with a flotilla of local fishing vessels, dinghies and other small craft, to pay their respects to *The Hampshire Rose*, as she made sweeps back towards the shore before making her way on her journey. The RAF Manston air sea rescue helicopter patrolled overhead as the lifeboat was escorted on the beginning of her journey, and the excited crowd were left to reflect on her departure.

Retirement from Walmer did not mean retirement from the RNLI, however. *The Hampshire Rose* was drafted into the RNLI relief fleet, and following some routine maintenance and a survey she was eventually sent to Anstruther Lifeboat Station, where they required substantial building works to their boathouse. Their Oakley class *The Doctors* was being replaced by a new Mersey class all-weather boat, and in the interim *The Hampshire Rose* was the ideal boat to cover the station, as it had been designed specifically for beach launching and did not need to be kept inside a station – after all, at Walmer she had sat quite happily on the beach for years!

The Hampshire Rose stayed at Anstruther from March 10th, 1991 until November 22nd of the same year, and during this period she was launched on service eight times.

The Hampshire Rose lying afloat during her time on relief at Anstruther Lifeboat Station

Following this 8 month period on relief in Anstruther, *The Hampshire Rose* travelled even further north to the Herd & Mackenzie shipyard in Buckie, where she was lifted out of the water. After some minor works, she began the long journey south to the RNLI depot at Poole, arriving on December 1st, where she was returned to the water ready to take up her next relief post.

Once back in the water, the lifeboat then continued on her journey, arriving on station at Swanage on December 2nd to begin a period as relief boat for their all-weather lifeboat, the Rother class *J. Reginald Corah*. In her six months on service at Swanage, she was launched six times, saving two lives.

The Hampshire Rose arriving in Poole on June 13th 1992

Returning to Poole on June 13th, 1992, *The Hampshire Rose* was then retired from service, after seventeen heroic years working for the RNLI.

After retirement, the lifeboat went onto the RNLI's sale list, and in October 1992 was sold to the first of a number of owners, for use as a pleasure boat. Around 2005, *The Hampshire Rose* was bought by a member of Ilfracombe RNLI's volunteer crew, and for a year she was run as a charter boat from the harbour, before being sold on again.

2006 saw her returning to Portsmouth. Thirty one years after being handed over to the RNLI at HMS Vernon, local press reported that the boat would take up a home berth at Gunwharf Quays – the site where the now closed HMS Vernon once stood.

The timing of her return was fortuitous, as Sir Alec Rose's yacht, *Lively Lady*, was being prepared for her newest adventure, a repeat of the famous world circumnavigation that Sir Alec had undertaken in 1967. The famous yachtsman had expressed a wish that his vessel work out her days, being used to make a difference to disadvantaged young people, and this journey was doing exactly that.

On 28th July, 2006, *The Hampshire Rose* was given the honour of escorting *Lively Lady* out of Gunwharf Quays as the yacht began the first leg of her around the world trip. With a naval band on board, and beautifully dressed for the occasion, the lifeboat, along with a

The Hampshire Rose carried a naval band who played as Lively Lady began her journey.

small flotilla of other craft, saw the famous sky blue yacht on her way.

On 3rd October 2006, another historic occasion in the life of *The Hampshire Rose* occurred. Members of the original fundraising committee gathered at Gunwharf Quays to officially welcome her back to the place where her story had begun over thirty years before.

For the first time ever, the committee members were able to go aboard the lifeboat and take a trip all together, and although their chairman, Sir Alec, was no longer with them, they certainly felt his presence on that day.

During Portsmouth Lifeboat Station Open Day 19th August 2007

During her time in Portsmouth, *The Hampshire Rose* was run as a charter boat, doing trips, day charters and events. She made guest appearances at some of Portsmouth RNLI Lifeboat Station's open days, appearing afloat with their two inshore lifeboats, and offering trips in aid of the charity.

Following several successful years at Portsmouth, *The Hampshire Rose* sadly began to be used less and less, and eventually the owner made the decision to sell her. In October 2012, she arrived in Ilfracombe and work began to restore her in order that she could begin the next stage in her charter boat life.

Arrival of The Hampshire Rose in Ilfracombe, Saturday 27th October 2012

Although the boat had been kept in good condition during her working life, the months of sitting on a mooring without use had taken their toll, and there was work to be done before she went back in the water and was put to work again. Most of this work was cosmetic, with every inch of her needing new paint, but there were a few bigger jobs to be done. The biggest by far was to replace the rear deck, which already had a panel missing on the starboard side and the remaining panels were rotting in many places.

Removing the deck panels was the first task, and the quality of the original build made this more difficult than it might otherwise have been. Every panel was screwed to the stringers below, with screws every inch or so, but they had also been stuck fast and then every join had been made watertight. Not only that, but the wheelhouse went over the top of the three centre panels, creating the bench seat inside.

The process of replacing the deck was a long one, weather dependent and time sensitive.

The missing panel made a good template, and although it was hoped that each panel would come out in turn to give us a template to cut a replacement, this was not to be. Much of each panel came apart where it was rotten, and along the stringers it was so well stuck it would not be removed. Rather than using the panels themselves as templates, we used the holes they left behind to achieve the task, but even this could not be done without preparation work. The old deck had to be sanded off the stringers as we went, meaning we were then able to fit the cardboard template pieces in well enough to ensure everything would fit tight.

Lifeboatman aims to restore old vessel for pleasure trips

By JOEL COOPER

A MAN who has crewed Ilfracombe lifeboat for more than 20 years has purchased an old lifeboat which he is hoping to bring back to life.

Lifeboat enthusiast Stuart Carpenter, 37, is hoping to offer unique boat trips on the 37-foot former RNLI Rother class vessel called The Hampshire Rose.

Stuart, who is an RNLI mechanic and helmsman and has crewed Ilfracombe lifeboat since he was 16, bought the ship in October last year.

He said: "She was built in 1975 and served from then until 1990 at Walmer in Kent.

"The Queen Mother attended her naming ceremony and famously dropped her handbag in the sea. A navy officer had to dive in and get it for her.

"She was named the Hampshire Rose after the famous sailor Sir Alec Rose who led the fundraising appeal for her."

From 1990 to 1992 she formed part of the RNLI relief fleet but after that she went into private ownership.

Stuart said: "Only 14 of these were built and just three are currently for sale."

In a bizarre coincidence, the Hampshire Rose was previously owned by former Ilfracombe lifeboat coxswain Dave Paul Clements.

Stuart said: "He sold it to someone in Portsmouth seven years ago.

"This person didn't use it as much as they thought they would and put it up for sale.

"I'm a real lifeboat enthusiast and as soon as I saw it I knew I wanted it."

Stuart, who also works as a manager of Denmans Electrical wholesalers, said the boat is mechanically sound but in dire need of painting and restoration.

He said: "We are going to replace part of the rear deck and repaint it in lifeboat colours.

"It's been hard work, some parts of the boat have 16 layers of paint on them.

"Fortunately I've had a lot of help from several fellow lifeboat crew members who have been great."

Stuart is planning to offer half hour pleasure cruises on the boat which will include sightseeing information as well as a history of the boat.

He said: "I love lifeboats and I thought this would provide something a bit different to the wildlife, fast-thrill or diving trips which are offered in Ilfracombe.

"It makes business sense and also appeals to me personally.

"It's a niche market but who wouldn't want to have a trip on a nice old lifeboat? It looks just like the old toy boats you used to play with in the bath."

The Hampshire Rose is due to be lifted into Ilfracombe Harbour on March 24 and Stuart hopes to start offering trips around Easter.

■ BOAT: Lifeboatman Stuart Carpenter with his purchase.

■ MAKING WAVES: The Hampshire Rose when it was in use.

■ MAPPED OUT: Stuart with the boat's plans.

Local North Devon journalist, Joel Cooper, contacted us during the overhaul of The Hampshire Rose. He wanted to write an article about the project, and in January 2013 he interviewed Stuart about the boat and his plans. On 31 January 2013, the article appeared in both the North Devon Journal (shown above), where Joel Cooper is Head of Content, and in their sister publication, the Western Morning News (headline and photo shown below).

Photographs by Mike Southon.

Labour of love as Stuart aims to revive old lifeboat

Former lifeboatman helps Hampshire Rose bloom again

An RNLI mechanic and volunteer crew member from Devon, with a passion for lifeboats, has renovated Walmer lifeboat station's former rescue boat the Hampshire Rose.

Stuart Carpenter, 37, who has crewed Ilfracombe lifeboat for more than 20 years, bought the 37ft Rother class wooden vessel in October aiming to offer boat trips. His business is now afloat, with just the signwriting to be completed.

He said: "I love lifeboats and am a real lifeboat enthusiast, so as soon as I saw it I knew I wanted it. The restoration has been hard work, as some parts of the boat had 16 layers of paint on them.

"I thought she would provide something a bit different to the wildlife, fast-thrill or diving trips which are offered in Ilfracombe. It makes business sense and also appeals to me personally. It's a niche market but who wouldn't want to have a trip on a nice old lifeboat? It looks just like the old toy boats you used to play with in the bath."

He said: "She was built in 1975 and served from then until 1990 at Walmer. She was named the Hampshire Rose after the famous sailor Sir Alec Rose who led the fundraising appeal for her."

Stuart, who also works for an electrical wholesaler, has

The renovated Hampshire Rose at its new home in Ilfracombe, Devon, where the owner offers sea tours in the historic lifeboat

been busy researching the history and added that from 1990 to 1992 she formed part of the RNLI relief fleet but after that she went into private ownership.

The Hampshire Rose was the last big lifeboat to stand on the foreshore at Walmer Green, a proud landmark for the seafront scene on The Strand. The craft had two diesel engines, a speed of eight knots and she carried a crew of seven.

Stuart would like to hear from Mercury readers with information, pictures or memories about his boat when it was based at Walmer lifeboat station. Contact him at Langleigh Country House, Langleigh Road, Ilfracombe, Devon EX34 8EA. His email address is www.lifeboattrips. co.uk or call 07818 094 228.

For more details visit his Facebook page The Hampshire Rose Lifeboat

---

Following January's local coverage, we were contacted by, Sue Briggs, a reporter for the East Kent Mercury. The North Devon Journal story had caught her attention, and she intended to run something similar. On 20 June, 2013, the above article appeared in the East Kent Mercury, and as a result of this article, we were contacted by several people who kindly sent photographs and their recollections of the lifeboat during her service life in Walmer.

Please note, the headline description of 'Former lifeboatman' is incorrect, as Stuart was and continues to be an active member of Ilfracombe RNLI's volunteer crew

All the work was taking place while *The Hampshire Rose* was on the car park in the harbour, open to the elements and subject to the bitterly cold temperatures of the winter. To attempt to combat the problem of rain, a scaffold structure was built and covered around her, but high winds meant that this became impractical and dangerous, so after just two weeks of protection, we were at the mercy of the weather once more.

Eventually, just under two months after starting work on the rear deck, it was complete and ready for painting. During the weeks spent on the deck, other work had been going on as well.

 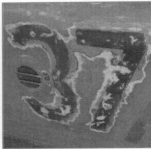

Taking the black vinyl numbers off the side (left) was the easy part, but it was what we found as we sanded off layers of paint that was interesting.

Several layers down were the original RNLI painted numbers (right) for the boat, and we used these as templates for the numbers we then attached.

In places there were as many as seventeen layers of paint, from traditional lifeboat orange to grey primers, and even two layers of yellow paint!

Scraping back the port deck in preparation for repair and then new coats of specialist deck paint

Every inch of the boat had to have old paint removed and surfaces prepared for a new paint job, and we used over 300 sanding discs and several tins of elbow grease to make that happen.

Due to the extremely cold weather of the winter, we were soon running out of time to paint her, as the surfaces of her hull were just too cold to allow the paint to dry properly. With a deadline of March 23rd, 2013 – lifting in day – we began becoming creative in

order to get the antifoul paint and blue hull paint on and dried. Using patio heaters to warm the surfaces, and keeping the paint in pans of hot water, we managed to achieve as fine a finish as we hoped for, and even succeeded in clawing back some of the time we had lost while waiting for the temperature to increase by a few degrees.

Patio heaters positioned around the hull during painting

All too soon, lifting in day arrived. From the decks down, the lifeboat was fully painted and ready, with the name and flag decals the only things to be finished off on her hull.

She had no new orange paint on her, but everything was prepared, ready for the coats of orange to go on.

The Hampshire Rose was ready to take to the water again.

The Hampshire Rose is lifted into the water at Ilfracombe for the first time since returning to the harbour in October 2012.

Top left: preparing to attach the crane's chains to the strops that have been run underneath the boat.

Top right: chains are attached, and bow and stern lines have been run so that helpers on the shore can keep her steady as she flies.

Bottom left: up, up and away!

Bottom right: splashdown. The Hampshire Rose is back in the water, crewed by volunteer RNLI lifeboat crew once more

The lifeboat makes her way out of Ilfracombe Harbour for her first journey under the control of new owner Stuart Carpenter, volunteer assistant mechanic for Ilfracombe RNLI, with the assistance of Andrew Bengey, volunteer Coxswain of Ilfracombe's Mersey class all-weather lifeboat.

On board for lifting in, and for the lifeboat's inaugural trip out of the harbour were members of Ilfracombe RNLI's volunteer crew. New owner Stuart Carpenter, volunteer assistant mechanic and helmsman for the charity, was joined by Andrew Bengey, volunteer Coxswain. Andrew had served on board Ilfracombe's Oakley class *Lloyds II* when she was in service, and although not identical, the classes were similar enough that this experience was invaluable when it came to the quirks of this lifeboat.

Heading for her moorings in Ilfracombe for the first time, with Damien Hirst's 'Verity' in the background

With more painting to be done before the season's trips could begin, there was no time to waste once *The Hampshire Rose* was in the water. The orange paint had all been stripped back to a smooth finish, and primed ready for the topcoats, but the temperature was still against us.

Finally, two weeks later, a beautifully sunny spring day, with the temperature finally into double figures meant that the first coat of orange paint could go on. The weather seeming to have turned in our favour then meant that it was all steam ahead, more coats of orange were applied, the final touches were added to the deck paint, and finally her vinyl name stickers and flags were applied to the hull

above: the vinyl stickers were added to the lifeboat's hull, and finally she was complete!

Sunday 19th May 2013, at 11.00, came the moment we had all been waiting for and working towards. Stuart took the boat off her moorings ready for her first day of trips *(right)*.

A full summer schedule followed, with trips running whenever the weather allowed. The fantastic weather of July and August, meant that there were people everywhere, and the chance of a trip aboard a lifeboat was too good for many to resist.

The arrival in the area of a bottlenose dolphin drew locals and tourists alike to the water. Performing for those aboard boats seemed to be the graceful mammal's strongest desire, and many of our passengers enjoyed an impromptu display from this playful creature.

Locally named 'Dave the Dolphin' leads The Hampshire Rose during an August trip.
Photo by George Slade

Although no longer an RNLI lifeboat, *The Hampshire Rose* is skippered, and often crewed, by members of the Ilfracombe RNLI volunteer lifeboat crew, who are always alert to the possibility of people in trouble.

On July 12th, 2013, two men on a jetski ran into difficulties with the craft close to the sightseeing route of *The Hampshire Rose*, as Stuart was out assessing the day's conditions. Upon being asked for assistance, he used one of his lines to rig a tow, and took the jetski's passenger aboard the boat.

As *The Hampshire Rose* was leaving the harbour on a tour in the afternoon of August 6th, 2013, skipper Matt Simpson, volunteer Deputy 2nd Coxswain for Ilfracombe RNLI, spotted two young men waving for help on Broadstrand Beach. The beach, at the base of Hillsborough, had become completely cut off by the incoming tide, and would soon be covered by the water. Matt radioed the coastguard and requested that the Ilfracombe RNLI lifeboat be launched.

On the request of the coastguard, *The Hampshire Rose* and her passengers then stood by until Ilfracombe RNLI's inshore lifeboat arrived and aided the stricken pair off the rocks and to the safety of the shore.

Finally, with a fantastic inaugural season behind us, on 10th November we were lifted back out of the water and placed back into our winter resting place, ready to start the off season work again and prepare for whatever the following year would bring.

The Hampshire Rose, having been lifted out of the water, is lowered onto her winter hard standing in the car park at Ilfracombe Harbour

Services of the Walmer Lifeboat RNLB *'Hampshire Rose'* – from Walmer Station archives

1975		
June 29th	Yacht *Shamrock*	Saved vessel, 2 people & 1 dog
Aug 8th	Yacht *Spanker*	Escorted vessel
Aug 11th	*Guya Franc*	Gave help
1976		
March 28th	Fishing vessel *Lady Jean*	Saved vessel & 6 souls
April 1st	Fishing vessel *Four Brothers*	Gave help
May 31st	Cabin cruiser *Phase II*	Saved vessel & 3 souls
May 31st	Cabin cruiser *Raven*	Gave help
Aug 4th	Cargo vessel *Mary M*	Stood by vessel
Aug 7th	Sloop *Romaphin*	Gave help
Aug 26th	Motor cruiser *Anjocyn III*	Gave help
Sept 1st	Yacht *Ay Bee Gee*	Gave help
1977		
May 7th	Escorted two vessels	
May 29th	Motor boat *Chips*	Saved vessel & 7 souls
May 29th	Yacht *Larissa*	Saved vessel & 3 souls
June 11th	Cabin cruiser *Popeye*	Landed 2 people
July 9th	Cabin cruiser *Up and Under*	Saved vessel & 3 souls
Oct 4th	Yacht *Helene*	Saved vessel & 2 souls
Dec 10th	Cargo vessel *Elmela*	Gave help
Dec 11th	Cargo vessel *Elmela*	Stood by vessel
1978		
April 8th	Yacht *Margalea*	Saved vessel & landed 3 people
April 30th	Fishing vessel	Gave help
1979		
June 5th	Yacht *Hendrick Jan*	Saved vessel & 4 souls
1980		
March 17th	Fishing vessel *Seafarer*	Gave help
Apr 26th	Motor boat *North Star*	Gave help
Jun 18th	Yacht *Vesta II*	Saved vessel & 3 souls
Jun 18th	Sailing surf boat	Landed 1 person
July 1st	Yacht *Zonne*	Saved vessel & 3 souls
July 17th	Cabin cruiser *Cookham Lady*	Saved vessel & 4 souls
Sept 15th	Yacht *Nikello*	Gave help
Sept 27/28	Trawler *Atlantic*	Gave help
Dec 17th	Motor boat *Sea Hooker*	Saved boat & 3 souls
1981		
June 16th	Motor boat *Golden Harvester*	Gave help
July 3rd	Yacht *Scarlet Lady*	Saved vessel
Aug 29th	Yacht *Torito*	Saved vessel & 3 souls
Sept 19th	Cargo vessel *Sanam*	Gave help

1982		
April 14th	Escorted two vessels	
June 7th	Motor boat *Sea Mist*	Gave help
June 22nd	Catamaran *Llara*	Gave help
July 24th	Rubber dinghy	Gave help
Aug 4th	Yacht *Kortgene*	Gave help
Aug 9th	Yacht *Herman*	Gave help
Aug 13th	Tug *Pacific*	Gave help
Sept 6th	Motor yacht *Compass Rose*	Gave help
Nov 21st	Dinghy	Saved boat & 4 souls
1984		
Feb 2nd	Trawler *Anne Elizabeth*	Gave help
Aug 16th	Yacht *Double Inn*	Escorted vessel
Aug 16th	Yacht *Surolu*	Gave help
Aug 16th	Yacht *Sweetheart*	Rescued 2 people
Dec 29th	Trawler *Opportunity*	Gave help
1985		
March 31st	Hovercraft	Recovered wreckage
April 28th	Yacht *Aellopos*	Gave help
Aug 11th	Yacht *Barcarale III*	Gave help
1986		
July 5th	Yacht *Gavia*	Gave help
July 31st	Motor vessel *Lagan Lomea*	Gave help
Aug 29th	Motor vessel *Shadow*	Gave help
Sept 4th	Sailing vessel *Gizmo*	Gave help
Sept 7th	Cabin cruiser *Panache*	Gave help
Oct 22nd	Sailing vessel *Outlaw*	Saved craft & 3 souls
Nov 18th	Vessel *Winston Churchill*	Landed injured man
1987		
April 18th	Yacht *Skald*	Gave help
April 26th	Fishing vessel *Zane Grey*	Gave help
May 10th	Cabin cruiser *Crown Jewel*	Gave help
July 6th	Fishing vessel *Freyer*	Gave help
Sept 27th	Cabin Cruiser *Shandra*	Gave help
1988		
Jan 10th	Motor vessel *Cornishman*	Escorted craft
1989		
Mar 25th	Cabin cruiser *Khadine*	Gave help
Oct 12th	Cabin cruiser *Cleopatra*	Escorted craft
Oct 26th	Yacht *Happy Morning*	Gave help
Dec 10th	Motor vessel *Pugwash*	Gave help
1990		
April 21st	Motor vessel *Kraken*	Saved craft & 2 souls

On relief at Anstruther: 8/0, Swanage:6/2
During 2013 season in Ilfracombe, towed 1 jetski and was involved in Ilfracombe RNLI's rescue of 2 boys cut off by the tide

This book would not have been possible without the generosity and assistance of several people.

Mr. B. Beer: www.eastkent.freeuk.com/deal/farewell.htm

Ms. S. Briggs, formerly of the East Kent Mercury

Mr. L. Coe, volunteer boathouse manager and ex – Head Launcher at Walmer RNLI Lifeboat Station.

Ms. J. Gaunt of Deal

Mr. P. O'Sullivan of Ramsgate

Mr. G. Smith of the East Kent Mercury

Mr. P. Stanford of Cheltenham

Mrs. S. Travis of Deal

Mr. C. Varrall, volunteer crew member at Walmer RNLI Lifeboat Station.

Mr. A. Worwood, volunteer shore helper and ex –crew member of The Hampshire Rose at Walmer RNLI Lifeboat Station

Mrs. G. Woods of Deal

Photographs from the archives of the late Basil Kidd have been used with the kind permission of his son, Mr. Nick Kidd. These photographs are to be found on pages: 22, 23, 25 – 28, 33, 34, 38, 39 and both the front and back covers.

Thanks to the East Kent Mercury, the North Devon Journal and the Western Morning News for the use of articles from their archives.

Some of the newspaper articles and photographs featured have been passed on to us. Despite our best efforts, we have been unable to match all of them to the newspapers they originated from, or the photographer, and thus they have not been attributed here.

Our deepest thanks also must go to all of those friends and family who offered time and effort to make this venture work. All of those who spent hours working on her during the cold days of the winter, everyone who gave their time to run her during the summer, and all of those who have been there every step of the way with advice, help, hot drinks and support. We could not have done this without you.